Rahim's Meta Model and the Management of Intra and Inter-Party Conflicts in Nigeria

Micheal Oluwasegun Aregbesola

i

DEDICATION

This book is dedicated to my MOTHER, who took loans for five years to see me through my undergraduate study successfully at the University of Ibadan. I honour your sacrifice to see me become a value to the society. I honour your faith in the promises of God concerning me and the steadfastness you have continued to demonstrate in my journey of BECOMING.

Thank you, mommy!

ACKNOWLEDGEMENT

I am grateful for the guidance, timely responses and constructive criticisms of Dr. Mrs Emordi who supervised this research from start to finish and helped in narrowing the focus of the problem this book addressed. My warm appreciation is also extended to Mrs S.B. Aregbesola who passionately supported me morally, physically, by typing the manuscript of this book and granting me a decent workspace all through the research writing stage. I am immensely grateful for your support.

TABLE OF CONTENTS

Introduction

The quest for the capture and control of political power is the basis for the existence of political parties. The relationship between parties, therefore, takes their cue from this basic consideration. As a result, it can be asserted that political parties have been part and parcel of political organisation since the creation of the nation state and are therefore pre-eminent institutions of modern democratic governance. Reputed as the "makers" of democracy, in an ideal setting, political parties basically are expected to serve as a formidable democratization force by articulating and aggregating public opinion and interests, engendering popular participation, contribute to the accumulation of political power, facilitate recruitment of political leadership, promoting political education and serve as a unifying force in a divided polity (Maiyo, 2008).

On the other hand, Key (1964) posits that political parties lie at the heart of democracy, representing the crucial link between what citizens want and what government does (Key, 1964 cited in Eme and Anyadike, 2011). That is why parties are trying continually to change, adapt, and adjust to the popular forces of their time. Across the globe, they want to stay in touch with the voters so that they can gain control of government and the policy making processes. This instance has been very pivotal to party pluralism which of course, lend a modicum of credibility to party competition and enhancing citizen's choice of party affiliation.

Party pluralism had first emerged in sub-Saharan Africa during the final stages of the colonial period, on the eve of independence, in the late 1950s and early 1960s. During the early 1990s, when we had the emergence of an African version of the global "third wave" of democratisation processes, virtually all sub-Saharan countries shifted from army-dominated or single-party-dominated regimes to formally democratic systems. Unsurprisingly, structural limitations (such as widespread and extreme poverty, low literacy levels, or state weakness), established political practices (notably, authoritarian rule and corruption) and the freshness of political reforms in these countries raised legitimate doubts about the depth of 'democratic' change (Giovanni, 2007). The latter, in many cases, was in fact limited to make up exercises. Overall, however, reforms undoubtedly brought about a significant return of multi-partism in sub-Saharan Africa (Giovanni, 2007).

With the end to military interregnum in Nigeria, the country once again returned to multiparty democracy in 1999, following the transition inaugurated and successfully completed by General Abdulsalam Abubakar. Initially, three political parties-the People's Democratic Party (PDP), the All People's Party (APP), later the All Nigerian People Party (ANPP), and the Alliance for Democracy (AD) were registered by the Independent National Electoral Commission (INEC) (Omotola, 2004). By December 2002, the number of registered parties rose to thirty, while an additional three political parties were registered in January-February 2006 (Antonia, cited in Omotola, 2010). In contrast however, in line with section (78) (7) (ii) of the electoral act 2010 as amended, which states that *'the commission shall have power to de-register political parties for failure to win a seat in the National or State Assembly election'* (Electoral Act, 2010), INEC de-registered 28 political parties on Dec 6, 2012. This was corroborated by the argument that these parties do not meet the standard requirement in terms of electoral performance and are therefore mushroom parties who have simply constituted a cog in the wheel of effective party politics in Nigeria.

Thus, the inherent weaknesses of political parties to enforce rule-based politics both within the party and the larger governance context lends credence to the need to investigate the nature and dynamics of intra and inter-party conflicts that have characterized Nigeria's Fourth Republic focusing on the second and third phase of the republic which experienced many battles in party politicking. More fundamental is the need to investigate the critical challenges responsible for poor conflict management amidst political parties and how to enhance the prospects of effective and cordial party relations in Nigeria. This is where this book is very dynamic as it examined the Rahim Meta Model of handling inter-personal conflict and applied the basics of the model to interpret party conflict from 2007 to 2011 in Nigeria and how best to enshrine democratic stability through proper conflict management practices.

CHAPTER ONE

Conceptual Overview and Literature Review

Conceptual Overview

Clarification of basic terms in a research endeavour remains pivotal to dispel any cloud of myth and doubts on the basic terms involved. For this book, the basic concepts that will be clarified in line with this book's intent are democracy, political party, conflict, conflict management and political stability. They are hereby clarified one after the other.

Democracy

Democracy is a concept that does not have any universally accepted definition. Despite the differences in conceptualization and practices, all version of democracy in the view of Osaghae (1992 in Lamidi and Bello,2013), share one fundamental objective of "how to govern the society in such a way that power actually belongs to all people". Democracy depends on parties to survive, since the structure of elections right from citizens participation to candidates' selection and presentation of competing political programmes is done by political parties. It is on this note that political parties occupy a special place in the democratic equation, and this is the position of this book.

Political Party

Appadorai in **The Substance of Politics (1968)** informs us that "A political party is more or less organized group of citizens who act together as a political unit, have distinctive aims and opinions on the leading political questions of controversy in the state, and who by acting together as a political unit, seeks to obtain control of the government". It is for this reason that it has been contended that perhaps more than any other factor, the success of democratic consolidation and political stability in a country is contingent on the effectiveness of political parties in structuring/managing political conflicts.

Conflict

While no single definition of conflict exists, most definitions involve the following factors: there are at least two independent groups, the groups perceive some incompatibility between themselves, and the groups interact with each other in some way (Putnam and Poole, 1987). This book sees conflict as the "process in which one party perceives that its interests are being opposed or negatively affected by another party" (Wall & Callister, 1995), and "the interactive process manifested in incompatibility, disagreement, or dissonance within or between social entities" (Rahim, 1992). Based on these definitions, the understanding of the basic goal of political parties as being solely focused on capturing power to control the machinery of government on the question of social direction and policy framework for common good makes the occurrence of conflict amidst them become inevitable.

Conflict Management

This study sees conflict management as the process of limiting the negative aspects of conflict while increasing the positive aspects of conflict. The aim of conflict management is to enhance learning and group outcomes, including effectiveness or performance in organizational setting (Rahim, 2002). Properly managed conflict can improve group outcomes. Conflict management does not imply conflict resolution. Conflict management minimizes the negative outcomes of conflict and promotes the positive outcomes of conflict from a gradualist perspective since conflict is not a 'one off' thing with the goal of improving learning in an organization while allowing challenge to the status quo which could easily serve as an obstruction to effective conflict management (Rahim, 2002). Therefore, it becomes paramount to understand how political parties have handled political conflicts and how this can be done in better ways to strengthen democratic practice and party politics in Nigeria.

Political Stability

According to this study, a polity can be said to be politically stable when and if there is a "congruence between the constitution and the regulatory rules of the system, such that changes within the action-set, either in terms of the realignment of forces in the set, or in its configuration, can be made to follow from and conform with the regulative rules of the system." Indeed, political stability is coterminous with political order and depends on the relationship between the level of political participation and the level of political institutionalization, which can be measured in terms of system maintenance, civil order, legitimacy, and governmental effectiveness (Dudley, cited in Omotola, 2010:126). From the foregoing, it can be asserted that the outcome of properly managed conflicts among political parties is political stability. As a result, it becomes crucial to explore how this can be attained in the Nigerian polity through functional conflict management techniques.

Literature Review

Often, political parties operate in line with conflicting circumstances which many times have generated violent conflicts in the polity. In this context, scholars analyse the operation and activities of political parties from different points of view. Atiku (2013) posited that internal party democracy backed by robust ideological orientation remains pivotal for peaceful party relation in Nigeria. In contrast however, Atiku asserted that rather than practice democracy in their internal affairs, what we have had is continuous deterioration in internal party democracy and the rise of the dictatorship of executive power-wielders, other party leaders and other godfathers. The military mindset is highly responsible for this. Interestingly, and quite unfortunately, this dictatorial command-and-control mindset had permeated executive-legislative interactions in Nigeria (Atiku, 2013).

In addition to the inherited mindset, another key challenge of internal democracy in parties is the structure of ownership of the parties. Nigeria's political parties are largely owned by godfathers rather than the mass of members and are largely run as personal fiefdoms even financed along these lines by owning godfathers, including governors, ministers, and other private individuals (Atiku, 2013:7). This is certainly not a recipe for democracy and as a consequence has generated intra-party bitterness and rumblings often giving rise to splinter groups, exit of some key members to other existing parties or formation of new parties (Nwolise, 2013).Corroborating the assertions above, Ojukwu and Olaifa, 2011, Aleyomi, 2013, Omotola, 2009, Lamidi & Bello, 2011, Anifowose & Akinbobola, 2005 have observed from all indications that the parochial idea of political party stalwarts in Nigeria is highly defective. Extensively, these scholars have deliberated at length on varying issues critical to internal party democracy and their consequence for inter-party conflict or peace dialogue for democratic stability in Nigeria. Some of these issues range from transparent party financial administration, imposition of candidates into elective position, indiscipline, party executive arrogance, zoning formula, rising magnitude of political vagrancy to poverty of party ideology strictly adhered to.

Critical to effective party relations is inter-party dialogue which must also focus on party reforms to creating an environment conducive to constructive intra-party dialogue. This is a matter of necessity considering the fact that if intra-party dialogue is not well compacted and managed, one cannot but expect that it will negatively impact inter-party dialogue (Jinadu, 2011).The justification for inter-party dialogue in Nigeria, taken alongside code of conduct for political parties and the provisions of the electoral law, as a matter of fact, will be helpful in conflict-prevention, conflict-management and confidence-building mechanism for bringing about cross-party cooperation for the consolidation and sustainability of democracy and development in Nigeria. Arguing differently from a radical view, (Omoweh, 2012) problematizes the democratization agenda of the Nigerian state and argues that the state's zero-sum politics block the process of democratizing development and the political parties from getting underway.

Furthermore, he opines that the contradictions inherent in the resistance of the elite, thrown up by the policies and politics of the state and the leadership of the parties are reviving pro-democracy agitations and revolutionary tendencies in Latin America and African countries. Consequently, he contends that the elite either democratize development process or risk mass action and revolution (Omoveh, 2012:55). In contrast however, revolution will be too costly. A mere act of revolution does not immediately transform to desired changes. The case of the Middle East remains a crucial lesson. Despite the Arab Spring that greeted the terrain in 2011/2012, many of the states affected are still battling with varying social and political conditions calling for serious attention. The end of revolution cannot be foretold hence the need for conflict management among political parties for democratic stability of the Nigerian state. The management approach gives a posture of a handy and effective style in addressing conflicting circumstances in the polity.

Conflict management must be viewed as part of a larger process of ensuring that man lives in peace and in an orderly way, conflict should also be channelled towards positive effect in every human community. Conflict management is another way of controlling conflict before or during and after it has occurred. According to Onigu Otite and Albert (1999:11), 'it is more elaborate and wider in conception and application, when necessitated; it involves conflict resolution and transformation. It is more of a long-term arrangement involving institutionalised provisions and regulative procedures for dealing with conflicts wherever they occur'. This view of the comprehensiveness and institutionalisation involved in conflict management is further stressed by Zartman (1989:8), when he wrote that 'conflict management refers to the elimination, neutralisation of conflict from erupting into crises or to cool a crisis in eruption'. Over the years the literature on conflict has reflected tensions between conflict management and conflict resolution. Now, however, the two issues seem to have been joined by the general acknowledgement that the process of conflict management can be an effective route towards conflict resolution (Aiyede, 2006:1).

While the varying issues of relevance reviewed above are largely internal to political parties, they are also a reflection of the broader problem of nation-building in Nigeria (Omotola, 2010). Thus, drawing heavily from experience since 1999 it is held that Nigerian political parties are yet to comprehend or appreciate its role in the task of national integration and nation building. Rather, the contradictions they engender do reinforce the integration crises (Abdulrasheed, 2007). Therefore, though the cross examination of the extant literature as reviewed above have dealt extensively on issues surrounding the relevance of political party in a polity, yet, despite these vast amounts of work, there remain a lacuna not explored over the years, and this is in regard of challenges responsible for poor conflict management among political parties with focus on how conflict management techniques or styles can be effectively used for productive party politics in Nigeria. In this, lies the uniqueness of this book.

CHAPTER TWO

Models of Conflict Management: An Overview

Early Conflict Management Styles

There have been many styles of conflict management behaviour that have been researched in the past century. One of the earliest, Mary Parker Follett (1926/1940) found that conflict was managed by individuals in three main ways: domination, compromise, and integration. She also found other ways of handling conflict that were employed by organizations, such as avoidance and suppression.

Blake and Mouton Model

Blake and Mouton (1964) were among the first to present a conceptual scheme for classifying the modes (styles) for handling interpersonal conflicts into five types: forcing, withdrawing, smoothing, compromising, and problem solving. In the 1970s and 1980s, researchers began using the intentions of the parties involved to classify the styles of conflict management that they would include in their models. Both Thomas (1976) and Pruitt (1983) put forth a model based on the concerns of the parties involved in the conflict. The combination of the parties' concern for its own interests (i.e., assertiveness) and their concern for the interests of those across the table (i.e., cooperativeness) would yield a particular conflict management style.

Pruitt called these styles yielding (low assertiveness/high cooperativeness), problem solving (high assertiveness/high cooperativeness), inaction (low assertiveness/low cooperativeness), and contending (high assertiveness/low cooperativeness). Pruitt argues that problem-solving is the preferred method when seeking mutually beneficial options.

Khun and Poole's Model

Khun and Poole (2000) established a similar system of group conflict management. In their system, they split Kozan's confrontational model into two sub models: distributive and integrative.

- Distributive - Here conflict is approached as a distribution of a fixed number of positive outcomes or resources, where one side will end up winning and the other losing, even if they do win some concessions.

- Integrative - Groups utilizing the integrative model see conflict as a chance to integrate the needs and concerns of both groups and make the best outcome possible. This model has a heavier emphasis on compromise than the distributive model. Khun and Poole found that the integrative model resulted in consistently better task related outcomes than those using the distributive model.

DeChurch and Marks's Meta-Taxonomy

DeChurch and Marks (2001) examined the literature available on conflict management at the time and established what they claimed was a "meta-taxonomy" that encompasses all other models. They argued that all other styles have inherent in them into two dimensions - activeness ("the extent to which conflict behaviours make a responsive and direct rather than inert and indirect impression") and agreeableness ("the extent to which conflict behaviours make a pleasant and relaxed rather than unpleasant and strainful impression").

High activeness is characterized by openly discussing differences of opinion while fully going after their own interest. High agreeableness is characterized by attempting to satisfy all parties involved. In the study they conducted to validate this division, activeness did not have a significant effect on the effectiveness of conflict resolution, but the agreeableness of the conflict management style, whatever it was, did in fact have a positive impact on how groups felt about the way the conflict was managed, regardless of the outcome.

Rahim's Meta Model

Rahim (2002) noted that there is agreement among management scholars that there is no one best approach on how to make decisions, lead or manage conflict. In a similar vein, rather than creating a very specific model of conflict management, Rahim created a meta-model (in much the same way that DeChurch and Marks, 2001, created a meta-taxonomy) for conflict styles based on two dimensions, concern for self and concern for others. The first dimension explains the degree (high or low) to which a person attempts to satisfy his or her own concern. The second dimension explains the degree (high or low) to which a person wants to satisfy the concern of others. These dimensions portray the motivational orientations of a given individual during conflict. Studies by Ruble and Thomas (1976) and van de Vliert and Kabanoff (1990) yielded general support for these dimensions. Combination of the two dimensions results in five specific styles of handling interpersonal conflict, as shown in diagram **1.0** below (Rahim & Bonoma, 1979).

Diagram 1.0

A Two-Dimensional Model of the Styles of Handling Interpersonal Conflict

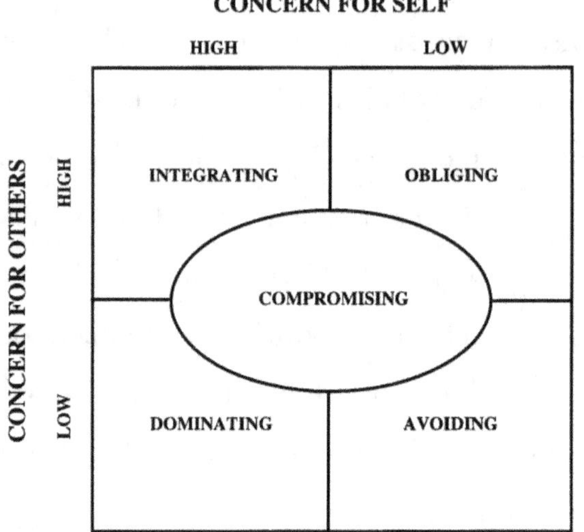

Source: Rahim, A., & Bonoma, T.V. (1979). Managing Organizational Conflict: A Model Diagnosis and Intervention. *Psychological Reports,* 44, 1327.

The styles of handling interpersonal conflict are described as follows.

1. *Integrating Style*

   This style indicates high concern for self and others. This style is also known as problem solving. It involves collaboration between the parties (i.e., openness, exchange of information, and examination of differences to reach a solution acceptable to both parties). "The first rule . . . for obtaining integration is to put your cards on the table, face the real issue, uncover the conflict, bring the whole thing into the open" (Follett, 1926/1940).

2.   *Obliging Style*

This style indicates low concern for self and high concern for others. This is also known as accommodating. This style is associated with attempting to play down the differences and emphasizing commonalities to satisfy the concern of the other party. These types of conflict strategies are indirect and cooperative (Blake and Mouton, 1964).

3.   *Dominating Style*

This style indicates high concern for self and low concern for others. This is also known as competing. This style has been identified with a win–lose orientation or with forcing behaviour to win one's position. The dominating style relies on the use of position power, aggression, verbal dominance, and perseverance. This style is direct and uncooperative (Blake and Mouton, 1964).

4.   *Avoiding Style*

This style indicates low concern for self and others. This is also known as suppression. It has been associated with withdrawal, buck-passing, sidestepping, or "see no evil, hear no evil, speak no evil" situations. It may take the form of postponing an issue until a better time or simply withdrawing from a threatening situation.

5.   ***Compromising Style***

This style indicates intermediate concern for self and others. It involves give-and- take or sharing whereby both parties give up something to make a mutually acceptable decision. It may mean splitting the difference, exchanging concession, or seeking a quick, middle-ground position. This style may be of some use in dealing with strategic issues, but heavy reliance on this style may be dysfunctional (Lee, 2008).

In the next chapter, I examined intra and inter party factors challenging parties' ability to manage conflict in Nigeria and the application of Rahim's meta model of handling inter-personal conflict and how it can enhance sustained virile party politics in Nigeria.

CHAPTER THREE

Challenges of Conflict Management and the Relevance of Rahim's Meta Model in Managing Party Conflicts in Nigeria

Intra-Party Factors Challenging Parties' Ability to Manage Conflicts in Nigeria, 2007- 2011

In Nigeria's Fourth Republic, party politics has been fraught with a lot of challenges that have threatened the foundations of Nigeria's democratic system both at the intra and inter-party levels. The intra-party challenges discovered within the timeframe of this research include the following:

Weak Legal and Institutional Framework including relationship with INEC

The liberalization of political party regime has led to the increase of parties with many of them being mushroom parties. Going by this truth, the 2010 Electoral Act gave INEC the power to de-register party and INEC used this power on 18th August 2011, to de-register seven parties that did not contest for any election office in the 2011 elections. They are the Democratic Alternative, National Action Council, National Democratic Liberal Party,

Masses Movement of Nigeria, Nigeria People's Congress, Nigeria Elements Progressive Party, and the National Unity Party (Daily Trust, 2011in UNDP, 2013). This phenomenon led to series of litigation charges and resentment from the de-registered parties against other parties in the polity. As touching relationship, the Independent National Electoral Commission (INEC) and the State Independent Electoral Commissions have powers under the Electoral Act 2010 to be present at conventions, congresses, conferences, or meetings of political parties as monitors to ensure that the parties respect their procedures.

In the 2011 elections, however, parties were able to disregard the role of INEC and do as they please, by marginalizing INEC under a barrage of court injunctions. At the party congresses, leaders were elected, and candidates were nominated for elective positions. The elections were however pre-determined at most times and party bosses tended to have the final say in the selection of leaders (UNDP, 2013). This is the underlying logic that has led to the process of continuous internal party crisis in the country.

Fluidity

In Nigeria, party membership is ephemeral as people engage the political process as patrons or as clients (UNDP, 2013). This means the attachment of people is not really to political parties but to patrons or godfathers who pay for their engagement. The implication of this is that participation in political party activities is mediated by political bosses to whom people owe allegiance. In Nigeria, Party life is most active around election time and patrons and godfathers engage in party activity to obtain nomination and elections for themselves or their surrogates. When they fail to obtain the position, they tend to move out with their clients to other parties in search of new opportunities. This was why Atiku moved out of PDP in 2007 to join other people in the formation of Action Congress (AC). The same thing happened to Muhammadu Buhari, leaving ANPP to form CPC in 2009 in preparation for the 2011 elections (Mamah, 2010 in Ogunne, 2011). In Nigeria therefore, both for the patrons and their clients, adherence to political parties is very fluid and opportunistic. It is also true that many people own multiple party cards as they seek to be invited to as many party congresses as possible where the tradition is to pay participants for their votes. Such people therefore move from party to party in search of opportunity. When instances like this surface, it limits party's ability in managing intra-party affairs.

Ideology and Issue Based Politics

The ideology question and the left/right divide have largely disappeared from Nigerian political parties, so conflicts are focused on the issue of personalities, ethnic groups, geopolitical zones, religion, and the control of power (UNDP, 2013). "Due to unclear cut ideology, politicians behave like political bats changing party affiliation" (Aina, 2002 in Lamidi & Bello, 2013). Within the period in review, the activities of all the parties shows that they possessed non identifiable ideology that serve as motivating force, which is expected to be the source of their manifesto (Ajetunmobi and Kehinde, 2007 in Lamidi &Bello, 2013). They failed to have a grand strategy of enlightening the electorates that would make them secure peoples votes. For instance, in 2007 the most visible message of the Action Congress (AC) campaign is that a vote for AC is a vote against the PDP government. The Democratic People's Party (DPP) presidential candidate promised free compulsory education for all if elected president; given that Sokoto state where he was their Governor then, has one of the highest illiteracy levels in the country.

Similarly, the PDP promises to make Nigeria one of the 20 greatest economies by the year 2010 (NDI, 2007b in Lamidi & Bello, 2013). It is deduced that most of the candidates failed to address fundamental questions of Nigeria's development. The focus of the campaign basically revolved around personality of the candidates. That made it difficult to distinguish between the sixty-three (63) registered political parties in 2011 in terms of ideology and policy. It may, therefore, be correct to assert that the first and most important vehicle of a political party, under an ideal situation, should be its ideological stance. However, the lack of this powerful instrument in controlling the internal dynamics of individual party, places serious threat to effective management of party conflicts in Nigeria.

Lack of Civility, Candidate Imposition and Exclusionary Politics
Civility is one quality that is largely absent in political party life. Thugs, violence, and betrayal are often the currency for political party engagement. Indeed, the period leading to each election is marked by the assassination of party leaders and contestants for various offices (UNDP, 2013). On the case of candidate selection, the process of nominating party flag-bearers at various levels of governance in the 2007 general elections, especially the presidential and gubernatorial elections, provided the worst-case scenarios (Omotola, 2010). In 2007, Musa Yar'Adua was single-handedly imposed on PDP by Obasanjo as his successor. The act caused a lot of party faithful to defect to other parties. Atiku was forced to leave the party for Action Congress (Aleyomi, 2013). A notorious instance of what happened between Rotimi Amaechi and Celestine Omehia as well as Ifeanyi Ararume of Rivers and Imo states respectively readily come to mind in this regard. Their names were substituted within the electoral body simply because they were not the godfather's favourite (Aleyomi, 2013; Omotola, 2010).

According to Ibrahim (2011), CPC leaders replaced gubernatorial candidates who had been successful in the Kano and Katsina primaries and instead installed candidates chosen by national party leadership. These internal conflicts over primaries left the party disorganized and factionalized, perhaps contributing to its poor performance in the 2011 gubernatorial elections. The imposition of Bamanga Tukur as the PDP chairman is against the tenets of intra-party democracy. The imposition was against the wish and consent of the people who had already voted Babayo *ab initio* as the representative from the Northeast zone, where PDP had zoned it Chairmanship to. Babayo won the zonal primaries but when it got to the PDP national convention his victory at the zonal level was set aside and he was short-changed (Aleyomi, 2013). Instances like these create rancour, displeasure and tensed situation within the rank and file of the party hence, limiting the prospects of managing conflicts peacefully.

Inter-Party Factors Challenging Parties' Ability to Manage Conflicts in Nigeria, 2007-2011

Nigeria's Political Party System

Nigeria operates as a one party dominant political system in which the dominant party controls enormous resources compared to the others. At the beginning of the Fourth Republic, only three political parties were registered, but the Supreme

Court decision allowed for the liberalisation of the regime and many more parties were registered. There are three categories of political parties – the dominant party on its own, parties with parliamentary representation and the other small parties most of which were established as possible platforms for important politicians that lose out in the bigger parties or to access resources from the electoral management body (UNDP, 2013). Parties with executive seats are tightly controlled by the President and State Governors, and party leadership is at the beck and call of these executives who can change them at will. The implication of the foregoing is that the dominant party makes policies that are anti-opposition thereby constraining the ability of opposition parties in making constructive contribution to the governance processes in the state. Typical in this regard is the use of finance to curtail the ability of opposition parties in their respective state. Therefore, PDP has been able to deny ACN states the actual entitlement from the consolidated revenue. Overall, these set of development deter effective party relations in Nigeria as they conceive one another as archenemies with mutually exclusive goals. In this lies the 'do-or-die' nature inherent in party relations in Nigeria.

Competitiveness

Competitive party politics is weak as the ruling parties have often falsified the electoral game while the parties in opposition must narrow a political base and insufficient resources to effectively compete for power (UNDP, 2013). As a result, the PDP used all the paraphernalia of power within it might to rig the 2007 general elections. Even the elected President, Umaru Musa Yar'Adua accepted that the election was rigged. In the 2011 general elections, the important thing about the 2011 elections was that because of the perceived injustice on the part of the supporters of the CPC candidate, it led to post-election violence in the Northern States with devastating humanitarian consequences. The import of all these is the damage it brings to virile party relations in Nigeria.

Party Intolerance

While the 2011 election was at hand, political parties began their campaigns at both the Federal and state levels. The most significant issue that arose from this was the hostile attitudes of some state governors towards candidates of other parties. Most of the state governors made deliberate and desperate efforts to prevent their rivals from campaigning in their states. Just a week into the governorship campaigns, the Action Congress of Nigeria, ACN, was denied access to hold its presidential campaign rally initially planned for the IBB Public Square in Makurdi, the Benue State capital, forcing the party to shift the venue to Gboko. The party had earlier alleged that it was denied holding its presidential rally in Jigawa on February 21 on the excuse that the state Governor, Sule Lamido was also billed to host his rally on the same date (Durogbo, 2011in Ogunne, 2011).

Also, in Abakaliki, the Ebonyi State capital, Governor Martin Elechi equally placed hurdles on the path of the major rival party, the All Nigeria Peoples Party (ANPP), banning it from starting its national campaign in the state. Dr. Ogbonnaya Onu, the ANPP National Chairman and —a son of the soil, had earlier announced that the kickoff of the party 's presidential campaign would be in Abakaliki, the state capital. But Elechi alleged that the plan of the party was to destabilise the state. For Niger State, the state police Command refused to allow the North Central zonal rally of the Congress for Progressive Change (CPC) to hold in the state on March 3, 2011 (Ogunne, 2011). The trend later developed into open confrontations and bloodletting as situations got worse. The immediate impact of the summation of all these political maneuverings and barring of opposition parties to hold their campaigns at different chosen centers majorly by PDP governors engendered political parties to become more hostile to one another even ever before the election proper.

Exploring Rahim's Meta Model of Conflict Management: Relevance to Managing Political Party Conflicts in Nigeria's Fourth Republic

From thorough research, Rahim and Bonoma (1979), and Rahim (1983, 1985, 1986a, 2001) styles of handling interpersonal conflict on two basic dimensions: concern for self and concern for others, is among the most popular styles of handling conflict used in research. In fact, Rahim and Bonoma's (1979) model was based on Blake and Mouton's (1964) grid of managerial styles as well as the Thomas-Kilmann MODE instrument (1974). Specifically, Rahim and Bonoma confirmed and refined the factor structure of the managerial grid through contact with over 1,200 corporate managers across the United States (Rahim, 1983 in Lee, 2008).

This work leads them to identify five specific conflict styles as shown in diagram **1.0** above. Hence, out of diligent study, I have found Rahim's meta model of handling inter-personal conflict useful in creatively interpreting political party conflicts in Nigeria and how to enhance political stability through better management practices. This section deals with the application of Rahim's meta model of handling inter-personal conflict to political party conflicts in Nigeria and prospects for political stability, democratic consolidation, and sustenance over time. The following techniques are considered:

Integrating Style

In this mechanism, the first rule . . . for obtaining integration is to put your cards on the table, face the real issue, uncover the conflict, bring the whole thing into the open" (Follett, 1926/1940). This implies that there must be roundtable discussions to explore differences and thereby creating avenues for problem solving from different quarters of interest of the parties in question. What is novel about the idea of inter-party dialogue is the need to institutionalize and routinize it as a confidence- and consensus-building feature of the electoral governance process. The justification for inter-party dialogue in Africa has typically been that, taken alongside code of conduct for political parties and the provisions of the electoral law, it is an important conflict-prevention, conflict-resolution, and confidence-building mechanism for bringing about cross-party cooperation for the consolidation and sustainability of democracy and development (Jinadu, 2011). Importantly, to sustain virile inter-party dialogue for problem solving of party problems in Nigeria, the following are essential.

(i)   meetings among political parties, the election commission, and civil society representatives can build trust among the various elections' stakeholders.

(ii)   structured multiparty dialogue can prevent conflict and election violence. Conference of Nigerian Political Parties can be constitutionally strengthened to make it more reliable in promoting constructive relations among political parties in Nigeria.

(iii) dialogue platforms between political parties and EMBs are the best vehicle to prevent election violence. Monitoring agencies collaborating with political parties with openness on the part of political parties to relay issues is also vital to promoting effective management of differences among political parties. According to Prein (1976) suggested that this style has two distinctive elements: confrontation and problem solving. Confrontation involves open communication, clearing up misunderstanding, and analyzing the underlying causes of conflict. This is a prerequisite for problem solving, which involves identification of, and solution to, the real problem(s) to provide maximum satisfaction of concerns of contending parties. These ideals are essential in ensuring strong party politics in Nigeria.

Obliging Style

This style is accommodating in nature. It is associated with attempting to play down the differences and emphasizing commonalities to satisfy the concern of the other party. There is an element of self-sacrifice in this style. It may take the form of selfless generosity, charity, or obedience to another party's order.

This style essentially focuses on finding same interest for parties while trying to minimize the true feelings of conflict to satisfy other parties. Here, it can be posited that the similarity in interest for the purpose of reducing the chances for conflict usually serve as a "conflict absorber" through which a perceived hostile act among parties has low hostility or even positive friendliness on the part of another party (Boulding, 1962).

Okudiba Nnoli (2003) asserted that ideology is a very crucial aspect of politics, not only by serving as a cognitive structure for looking at society generally and providing a prescriptive formula, that is, a guide to individual action and judgement, but also as a powerful instrument of conflict management, self-identification, popular mobilization and legitimization. Instead of parties contributing to the building of state structures and the consolidation of development, they have been reduced to tools for promoting sectionalism and opportunism. All these attendant issues have therefore raised the stakes for Nigeria to return to the ideal of healthy party politics- the establishment of political parties on genuine ideological stance, if genuine intra and inter-party relations for sustainable conflict management will be ensured in Nigeria. Also, level playing field must be given to all political parties in terms of access to the media without any form of biases on the part of the media against some parties. The use of the media for incendiary comments by some parties against others within the same political system should not encouraged in the system to promote sustainable and healthy party politics in Nigeria.

Dominating Style

The dominating style has high concern for self and low concern for others. This is also known as competing. This style has been identified with a win–lose orientation or with forcing behaviour to win one's position. The zero-sum game of politics where winner takes all is the approach to politicking is well-founded on this basis. Examples of these are god-fathers and party politics, party executive arrogance, consensus candidature, discrimination against women and youth due to domination of party finances by elder –elite. Without mincing words, the archetypal godfather in Nigeria is more than the ruthless Mario Puzo's kingpins in the Italian Mafia setting. While the fictional godfather is characterized as 'a shadowy, dare-devil recluse, who combines immense underworld financial muscle with near mythical powers of enormous proportions', which is to attain a further greasing of the ever-increasing vast financial empire, the Nigeria type has the added characterization of conceit, ego, loquacity, pettiness, envy, strife, crudity, and confusion that worsen the prospects of peaceful conflict management among political parties (Albert, 2005). Richard Joseph described the phenomena of 'prebendalism' and 'clientelism' as two of the most important principles of political organisation and behaviour in Nigeria. Both are mutually reinforcing and affect and even determine the allocation of public goods in the country. The female politician is the major victim of the lack of civility in the political process. She suffers from various modes of marginalisation many of which are hurtful and full of invectives (Ibrahim and Salihu, 2004).

It is noteworthy that the dominating style relies on the use of position power, aggression, verbal dominance, and tenacity. This style is direct and uncooperative (Blake and Mouton, 1964). Within interpersonal context, the dominating (competing/distributive) style has been found to be associated with low levels of effectiveness and appropriateness. Therefore, party politics has been seriously dented in Nigeria and if there will be a turn-around of circumstances to promoting virile party politics in Nigeria, especially in effective conflict management, the fundamental objective of political party development should be to reverse this trend and get more people with ideas and vision to integrate the leadership of political parties.

Avoiding Style

The avoiding style is a zero-sum or negative-sum game. It indicates low concern for self and others. This is also known as suppression. It has been associated with withdrawal, buck-passing, sidestepping, or "see no evil, hear no evil, speak no evil" situations (Rahim, 2001). It may take the form of postponing an issue until a better time or simply withdrawing from a threatening situation. This scenario is well justified in the phenomena of party switching or defections and their consequent impact on creation of opposition parties, compounding the system' capability to manage emergent conflicts from the multiplicity of political parties within the polity without any sound ideological stance. In 2007, Musa Yar'Adua was single-handedly imposed on PDP by Obasanjo as his successor. The act caused a lot of party faithful to defect to other parties.

Atiku was forced to leave the party for Action Congress (Aleyomi, 2013). The same thing happened to Muhammadu Buhari, leaving ANPP to form CPC in 2009 in preparation for the 2011 elections because of the disappointment being meted out to him by the national executives of ANPP who accepted the offer of Yar'Adua to participate in the proposed Government of National Unity and whom he referred to as "political jobbers" as against Buhari's lawsuit against the fraudulent 2007 General Elections (Mamah, 2010 in Ogunne, 2011). Instances like the foregoing aggravate instability and compounds system's capability to manage conflicts. Though, it is important to state that it is not a crime to switch to another party if it is done on justifiable basis within the limits of the constitution. But the prevalence of this phenomenon in Nigeria has been seriously abused for selfish aggrandizement and to enhance prospects for effective political party conflict management, efforts must be gravitated towards best democratic practices that can enliven virile party politics in Nigeria.

Compromising Style

The compromising style indicates intermediate concern for self and others. It entails give-and- take or sharing whereby both parties give up something to make a mutually acceptable decision. It may mean splitting the difference, exchanging concession, or seeking a quick, middle-ground position. A compromising party gives up more than a dominating party but less than an obliging party. It is a mixed (no-win/no-lose) style. This implies that the cut-throat zero-sum game predominant in party politicking must be done away with. Opposition parties should be integrated by the incumbent party into the system of coordinate policy making and implementation to reducing prospects for unconstructive criticism- the backbone of unmitigated conflicts amidst political parties. Within the ambits of the foregoing, the scenario of Government of National Unity called for by late President Shehu Musa Yar'Adua in 2007 is relevant here.

A functional opposition is, to all intents and purposes, a "Shadow Government" and must function as such outside of government, rather than allowing itself to be co-opted into the government in power. However, in effect, the Nigerian opposition has abandoned Nigerians in the middle of our democratic journey. It's a betrayal of trust and confidence reposed in them by Nigerians. The Nigerian opposition, rather than collapsing itself into the ruling party, must proactively organize and make itself relevant in Nigeria's democratic march to playing its assigned role. The recent development with the All Progressives Congress (APC) is encouraging before its emergence as the ruling party in the 2015 general elections. In these lays therefore, the assertion that the integration mechanism, without much ado, remains pivotal to the sustenance of virile party politics in the Nigerian polity.

CHAPTER FOUR

Conclusion and Policy Recommendations

Conflict is inevitable in the political process since it epitomises divergent views and preferences, but the failure to use acceptable tools for the management and resolution of such a conflict, is detrimental to the growth of democracy and the political stability of Nigeria. Resolution of conflict through means other than dialogue portrays a very parochial and low political culture. It minimises the importance of elections in the democratic process. It also makes the competitive function of elections for the determination of political leadership irrelevant. It is therefore instructive that dialogue should be seen as the mechanism for the resolution of conflicting claims and positions through the electoral process. Without doubts, the dominating and avoiding styles are considered ineffective in managing conflict. The dominating style relies on the use of position power, aggression and tenacity thereby emphasizing godfatherism, party executive arrogance and discrimination against women and youths. As for avoiding style, it indicates withdrawal, buck-passing and sidestepping hence encouraging party switching or defection with the implication of compounding system's capability to manage emergent conflicts from the multiplicity of political parties within the polity without sound ideological stance.

Against this backdrop, within interpersonal context, dominating and avoiding styles have been found to be associated with low levels of effectiveness and appropriateness. From the other styles in the model, a deep and objective exploration of facts within the Nigerian polity reveals that the integration style remains the sine qua non in reviving virile party politicking in Nigeria. The integration style brought to limelight the relevance of uncovering conflicts, exploring differences, and creating avenues for roundtable discussions to explore differences in form of inter-party dialogue. The justification for inter-party dialogue is contingent on the fact that it is an important conflict-prevention, conflict-resolution, and confidence-building mechanism for bringing about cross-party co-operation for the consolidation and sustainability of democracy and development. In all seriousness, the desired community can only evolve through mutual tolerance and respect for every member of the political community. As a result, negotiation and problem-solving approach must be entrenched in the Nigerian polity through mutual consent of all stakeholders of the Nigerian project with die-hard commitment to make things works even in the face of compelling challenges. This is promotional in nature as it enhances centripetal forces as against centrifugal forces inherent in the avoiding style. Playing the game according to the rules of the game requires that all concerned should be law abiding. This then makes discipline not only desirable for every political aspirant, but indeed a definite necessity for the collective. Therefore, sustaining party discipline surely would be one way of minimising both intra-party and inter-party-political violence. It surely would be a way of promoting positive and enduring political socialisation.

Recommendations

Given the significant gaps in the party system and in political party capacity to manage conflicts at present, there are considerable opportunities for productive engagement but also immense difficulties in building initiatives that can have positive impact. If those initiatives challenge the interests of powerful "godfathers" within the parties and the political system at large. At both the party system level, and the level of the individual parties, there are several interventions which can have positive influence on increasing the democratic character of Nigeria's political processes. The following recommendations are worthwhile to sustain virile inter-party dialogue for solving party problems in Nigeria:

- Liaison meetings among political parties, the election commission, and civil society representatives can build trust among the various election's stakeholders. This should be earnestly encouraged for mutual discourses to serve as platform where contending issues can be brought to the front burner of national discourse to finding lasting solution through concerted efforts.

- Structured multiparty dialogue can prevent conflict and election violence. To be effective, this forum needs to bring all the parliamentary parties together at the table and ensure that both the ruling party and the opposition parties agree to take the issues raised at the forum seriously. Such a forum could help reduce electoral and political violence, develop an agenda for electoral reform and improved elections management, and build a culture of trust, tolerance, and acceptance of diversity in Nigeria's charged political climate. This forum would not necessarily replace the existing fora like Inter Party Advisory Council (IPAC) and Conference of Nigerian Political Parties (CNPP) but would complement them as a space to address issues that need the presence of all of Nigeria's largest parties, whether on electoral issues, conflict management, legal reform, policy dialogue, or reducing hostility between competing political parties. Contingent on this therefore, to ensure that the inter-party forums are adequately representing all Nigerians, parties should ensure that their delegations include significant numbers of women, youth, and persons with disabilities. The agenda for dialogue forums should also be inclusive to address electoral- and party-related concerns of particular interest to women, youth and PWD.

- It is also important to emphasize in this regard that to ensure conflict management among political parties in Nigeria; level playing field must be given to all political parties in terms of access to the media without any form of biases on the part of the media against some parties. The use of the media for incendiary comments by some parties against others within the same political system should not be encouraged in the system to promote sustainable and healthy party politics in Nigeria.

- Unproductive leadership coordination of political party affairs must be done away with. Therefore, party politics has been seriously dented in Nigeria and if there will be a turn-around of circumstances to promoting virile party politics in Nigeria, especially in effective conflict management, the fundamental objective of political party development should be to reverse this trend and get more people with ideas and vision to integrate the leadership of political parties. Leadership with vision and integrity to maintain diligent and workable party structure with zero tolerance to money-bag politics should be encouraged and supported to achieve sustainable peaceful relation among parties. As a result, massive orientation and re-orientation must be embarked upon by civil society organizations to divest the entrenched thought of money-bag politics in the hearts of party members and general populace bringing to their knowledge the long-term negative consequences of allowing their integrity to be bought with money both for themselves as individuals and the polity at large.

- Dialogue platforms between political parties and EMBs are the best vehicle to prevent election violence. Monitoring agencies collaborating with political parties with openness on the part of political parties to relay issues is also vital to promoting effective management of differences among political parties. According to Prein (1976) suggested that this style has two distinctive elements: confrontation and problem solving. Confrontation involves open communication, clearing up misunderstanding, and analyzing the underlying causes of conflict. This is a prerequisite for problem solving, which involves identification of, and solution to, the real problem(s) to provide maximum satisfaction of concerns of contending parties. These ideals are essential in ensuring strong party politics through commitment to achieving a stable polity by all concerned stakeholders in the Nigerian project.

REFERENCES

Abati, R. (2007). Yar'Adua's Government of National Unity. www.villagesquare.org. Retrieved, 06/03/2015.

Abdulrasheed, A.M. (2008). Intra-party Relations and Conflict in Nigeria. *Pakistan Journal of Social Sciences 5* (1): pp. 42-50.

Aiyede, E.R. (2006). Theories in Conflict Management. National Open University of Nigeria, pp. 2-3.

Akindele, S.T. (2011). Intra and Inter-Party Post-Election Crises/ Feud Management in a Pluralistic Democracy. An X-Ray of the Nigerian Political Landscape. *African Journal of Political Science and International Relations. Vol.5(6), pp.287-330.*

Albert, I.O. (2005). Explaining Godfatherism in Nigerian Politics. *African Sociological Review. Vol. 9, (2), 2005, pp.79-105.*

Aleyomi, M.B. (2013). Intra-party Conflicts in Nigeria: The Case Study of Peoples Democratic Party (PDP). *Journal of Sustainable Development in Africa.* Vol. 15:4, pp. 281-296.

Anifowoshe, R. and Akinbobola, A. (2005). Party Discipline and the Electoral Process in Nigeria's Fourth Republic (1999-2003). An Analysis of Problems and Prospects. Lagos Historical Review, Vol. 5. pp. 111-130.

Appadorai, A. (1968). The Substance of Politics. Oxford University Press.

Atiku, A. (2013). Thoughts on Internal Democracy in Nigerian Political Parties: Challenges and Strategies. Being a Lecture Delivered on March 13 in the Faculty of the Social Sciences, University of Ibadan in Honour of the Department of Political Science: Celebrating 50 Years of Dedicated Service to Nigeria and Humanity.

Biezen van, I. (2004). How Political Parties Shape Democracy: Perspectives from Democratic Theory, Birmingham, University of Birmingham.

Blake, R. R., and Mouton, J. S. (1964). The Managerial Grid. Houston, TX: Gulf.

DeChurch, L. A, & Marks, M. A. (2001). Maximizing the benefits of task conflict: The role of Conflict Management. *The International Journal of Conflict Management,* 12, 4-22.

Electoral Act, (2010). Federal Republic of Nigeria Official Gazette. 24th August, vol. 97, pp. 1103-1202.

Eme, O.I. and Anyadike, N. (2011). Intra and Inter-Party Crises in Nigeria's Fourth Republic: Implications for the Sustainability and Consolidation of Democracy in Post Third Term Nigeria. *Journal of Social Science and Public Policy, Vol. 3, pp. 38-52.*

Follett, M. P. (1940). Constructive Conflict. In H. C. Metcalf & L. Urwick (Eds.), <u>Dynamic Administration: The collected papers of Mary</u>

Parker Follett (pp. 30–49). New York: Harper & Row. (Originally published 1926).

Giovanni, M.C. (2007). Political Parties and Party Systems in Africa: Themes and Research Perspectives. *World Political Science Review, Vol. 3, Issue 3, pp. 1-4.*

Hague, R. and Harrop, M. (2007). *Comparative Government and Politics*, New York, Palgrave Macmillan.

Ibrahim, J. (2011). The Dynamics of Competitive Party Politics. In Ibrahim, J., Abutudu, M., and Kelechi C. Iwuamadi, (ed). Elections and the Management of Diversity in Nigeria, African Governance Report III.

Ibrahim, J. and Salihu, A. (2004). "Women, Marginalisation and Politics in Nigeria", Centre for Democracy and Development, Open Society Initiative and Global Rights, Abuja. Unpublished Paper.

INEC (2012). De-Registration of 28 Political Parties. www.inecnigeria.org. Accessed 12th February 2014.

Jinadu, L.A. (2011). "Inter-Party Dialogue in Nigeria: Examining the Past, Present and Future". Lead Paper at the Inaugural DGD Political Parties Dialogue Series, Held October 4, at Bolingo Hotel, Abuja.

Joseph, R. (1987). Democracy and Prebendal Politics in Nigeria: The Rise and Fall of the Second Republic, Ibadan: Spectrum Books.

Kirchheimer, O. (1966). The Transformation of the Western European Party System. In <u>Political Parties and Political Development</u>, (ed). J. La Palombra and M. Weiner (Princeton, NJ: Princeton University Press) pp. 177-200.

Kuhn, T. & Poole, M. S. (2000). Do conflict management styles affect group decision making? *Human Communication Research, 26, 558-590.*

Lamidi, K.O. and Bello, M.L. (2013). Party Politics and Future of Nigerian Democracy: An Examination of Fourth Republic.*European Scientific Journal, Vol. 8, No. 29, pp. 168-178.*

Lee, K.L. (2008). An Examination between the Relationships of Conflict Management Styles and Employees' Satisfaction. *International Journal of Business and Management. Vol.3 No. 9, pp. 11-25.*

Maiyo, J. (2008). Political Parties and Intra-Party Democracy in East Africa: From Representative to Participatory Democracy. A Thesis for Master of Philosophy in African Studies, Africa Studies Centre, Leiden University, pp. 1-13.

Ogunne, K.O. (2011). Political Parties Activities and Post-Election Violence in Northern Nigeria: Case Study of 2011 Presidential Election. A Long Essay Submitted to the Department of Political Science, Faculty of Social Sciences, Obafemi Awolowo

University, Ile-Ife, Nigeria; pp. 1-4, 25-27, 33-37. Retrieved 3/1/2014 from www.academia.edu.ng.

Ojukwu, E.C., and Olaifa, T. (2011). Challenges of Internal Democracy in Nigeria's Political Parties: The Bane of Intra-Party Conflicts in the People's Democratic Party in Nigeria. *Global Journal of Human Social Science, Vol. 11:3, pp. 24-34.*

Okechukwu, E.I. and Anyandike, N. (2011). Intra and Inter-Party Crises in Nigeria's Fourth Republic: Implications for the Sustainability and Consolidation of Democracy in Post Third Term Nigeria. *Journal of Social Science and Public Policy*, Vol. 3, pp. 38-52.

Omotola, J.S. (2008). Impeachment Threats and Nigeria's Democracy. In: Ojo, B.O. (*ed.*) Challenges of Sustainable Democracy in Nigeria. Ibadan: John Archers.

Omotola, J.S. (2009). Nigerian Parties and Political Ideology. *Journal of Alternative Perspectives in the Social Sciences, Vol. 1:3, pp. 612-634.*

Omotola, J.S. (2010). Political Parties and the Quest for Political Stability in Nigeria". *Taiwan Journal of Democracy, Vol. 6, No. 2: pp. 125-145.*

Omoveh, D.A. (2012). "Deconstructing the Democratic Developmental State: Blocked Democratization and Political Parties in Nigeria and South Korea". *Not Stated*

Osaghae, E. (1998). The Crippled Giants: Nigeria Since Independence. London: Hurst and Company.

Otite, O. and Albert, O. (eds). (1999). Community conflicts in Nigeria: Management, Resolution and Transformation. Ibadan: Spectrum books.

Otorofani, F. (2007). Proposed National Unity Government: The Red Flag Up. www.nigerianewspapers.com. Retrieved, 06/03/2015.

Philips, W.S. (1997). Power and Choice: An Introduction to Political Science. New York: McGraw Hill.

Prein, H.C.M. (1976). "Stijlen van conflicthantering [Styles of handling Conflict]". *Nederlands Tijdschrift voor de Psychologie, 31, 321–346.*

Pruitt, D. G. (1983). Strategic Choice in Negotiation. *American Behavioral Scientist, 27, 167-194.*

Rahim, M. A., & Bonoma, T. V. (1979). Managing Organizational Conflict: A Model for Diagnosis and Intervention. *Psychological Reports, 44, 1323-1344.*

Rahim, M., Antonioni, D., & Psenicka, C. (2001). A Structural Equations Model of Leader Power, Subordinates' Styles of Handling Conflict and Job Performance. *International Journal of Conflict Management, 12(3), 191.*

Rahim, M.A. (1992). Managing Conflict in Organizations (2nd Edition). Westport, CT: Praeger.

Rahim, M.A. (2002). Toward A Theory of Managing Organizational Conflict. *Journal of Conflict Management,* pp. 206-235.

United Nations Development Programme (UNDP) (2013). A Capacity Assessment of Nigerian Political Parties. Democratic Governance for Development (DGD), UNDP, Nigeria.

Wall, J.A., Jr. and Callister, R.R. (1995): Conflicts and Its Management. *Journal of Management,* pp. 515-558.

Zartman, William. (1989). Ripe for Resolution: Conflict and Intervention in Africa. Oxford: Oxford University Press.